Closest Pronunciation

THE DRINKING GOURD CHAPBOOK POETRY PRIZE

SERIES EDITORS

John Alba Cutler
Reginald Gibbons
Susannah Young-ah Gottlieb
Ed Roberson

Closest Pronunciation

Poems

Ed Roberson

NORTHWESTERN UNIVERSITY PRESS

EVANSTON, ILLINOIS

Northwestern University Press
www.nupress.northwestern.edu

Northwestern University Poetry and Poetics Colloquium
www.poetry.northwestern.edu

Printed in the United States of America

10   9   8   7   6   5   4   3   2

Library of Congress Cataloging-in-Publication Data
Roberson, Ed.
    Closest pronunciation : poems / Ed Roberson.
        p. cm. — (Drinking gourd chapbook poetry prize)
    ISBN 978-0-8101-2892-7 (pbk. : alk. paper)
    I. Title. II. Series: Drinking gourd chapbook poetry prize.
PS3568.O235C58 201
811.54—dc23

                                                        2012031401

♾ The paper used in this publication meets the minimum requirements
    of the American National Standard for Information Sciences—
Permanence of Paper for Printed Library Materials, ANSI Z39.48-1992.

Contents

Bend	*1*
The Hills	*2*
How Should This Be Read	*3*
How the Air Works	*4*
Deposition	*6*
Form at the Local Stage	*8*
Night Writing	*12*
Next to Nothing	*13*
Ghost Dance Song for the Bed Next to Mine	*14*
A Sky of Ceiling, a Lone Cloud Its Fan	*15*
Locus in Black Folktale	*16*
I Keep Arriving at a House That Isn't Mine	*17*
I Didn't Mean To Be	*18*
Gospel	*19*
Seated Woman	*20*
The Good Woman Forgives God His Being	*21*
Drawing the Hand	*22*
Was There	*24*
The Edge	*26*
Spring as the Comics Section	*27*
American Goldfinch	*28*
The Following Moment (Spain)	*29*
Transporte Mixto	*30*
Untitled	*31*
Instrument	*32*

Bend

(among twenty snowy . . .

that unfolds the road
through the pass has

that point where you leave
the whole side of one

mountain
back on the other side

for this one as
it's all of any side you can see

that simple   that
huge   one

migratory origami
fold

No one notices
your eye   a black history   have to do this.

The Hills

Coal piled in the hopper cars draws out
a low continuous ridge like one
from which it's stripped, scraping by
at the crossing in town, a horizon

so familiar I didn't see it end.
The pickups' horn chorus of those who did
see, focused no further than where they are
and on their way to just this side of that,

opens the lead for me, and I sing into gear
as usual not fully here but at the wheel.
We sing something   like, the hills
are forever, hill places that know our way.

The truck pulls off. Today, I have no way.
No shiny new shed skin, a sameness thickens
so opaque there are no markings anymore,
nothing's new but that the worn out seeing

has worn in. So close is our same to forever.
Though in the human hand of companies, we read
the hills roll away. We,
as graffiti on the cars' wall says, have lost. Our title.

How Should This Be Read

(poem with a line from M. Fateen)

A line of geese above a line
of cars on Lake Shore Drive
The crowns of trees below
a distant line of whitecaps

And closer   fluid chevrons
of parked tractor trailers
in the staging depot shifting
as the tide of deliveries

pulls them out and back—
stretches of
understood passage—   and not—rising and falling into place

between the two points that define
a line   a signing on   to itself
            to dwell
perpendicular to heaven
and parallel to hell

How the Air Works

how the air works with light
puddling that blue   sky into water pooled
in the heated dark above the surface
of the road   off that glance at itself

mirrored in the window of passing
how we adjust that spill of the heavens'
slip   glaze into an onyx keep of moving
the locket of our eyes only a memo

to lose weight stand up straight get a haircut
any order not a mirage the nonsense of
seeing assembled out of a whole lot
of what it's not any more than

what is capable of notice and we that
capacity   limited as   it is   are

---

the chairs and table obscured, camouflaged
within a thicket of spotted light, a shadow-
potted veranda, the house cat's nap catches
to play with   a twitch in its leopard sleep

---

i.e., cont'd

A bedsheet's wrinkles   imprinted on the skin
do the reverse of camouflage   the trail
of your location written out   uncovered in
the lines   a relief map that waking land opens,
mines with the undone   waiting and querulous

the polishing rags you've slept in
by design of your not doing
shine your sorry face
to its smooth excuse

_____

Deposition

low sun slides in
under a cloud layer   open to the west

shadows flatten down
stretched east   out across the tracks

at the edge of the rail
right-of-way   light broadsides the train

running north through—
shadows splash up the bank   of coaches.

flash cards   a bar code of shade trees flip up
on all that passes

through them
the sun-dazzled metal streams a momentary

rebuttal to vocabulary—
from the opposite of all direction: no, *here* is your sunset!
                                       no, here is the blotter of your sunset!

Out in the clouds, the panicked herd of heat
Lightning gallops back and forth corralled
Into the sky fenced by the earth into
Everywhere overhead.
                                    The animal
At the grounded mercy of what it can't hear,
But is coming, underneath what you hear.

The smell before storms that raises those hairs,
The ears. That lifts your head out of the crowd
Before the nose even catches on.
                                    A wind
Of which you can't see, of what if anything
There   except answer a full leap ahead of
Any question,   beyond push or shove.

Form at the Local Stage

The buzz of the old neon sign cut off
brightens the dark silence to the smell,
briefly, that odor of electricity.

Scent or day, both swiftly as a bell sound,
gone, closes and locks the door, the chime held
quiet.
          The sign always says *Open*,
the lights off say *Closed* in a common sense.
The definitive move, a blind gets rolled down.

The appearance that it all stood and left last night,
come morning, ready for their parts called back,
opens a last act with staying closed all day,

final curtain drawn by yellow police tape.
No performance announcement, a local set up
his tryout last night as a thief whose last lines cut the stage lights out.

Last night we'll say was tragedy we'll say was fire
between the first and second scrim of the skyline.
Too dark for fog, so it *was* smoke I saw,
smoke lit from beneath like
the cloud home to roost on a smokestack overnight
above the laying lights of a factory.
Instead of production line whistles clucking there
were sirens in an unseen orchestra.
A trap below what burns to the ground onstage
provides unseen entrance and exit
to the change ready to come of is
what's left.
what's left.   I've never understood
why applause
counts at the precise point that what doesn't matter
is the audience. It's too late
to listen.

A sunset comes back in the middle of the night,
but its reds are the lights of an ambulance
silently pulled up outside.   The walls wake

and windows—open floors above,
having seen directly down into the dark—
                    widen to that silence which is more

void than noiselessness   that sets
as horizon   un-pointed edges of the world
as the glowing bar to sail over: or window sill to

below   fifteen apartment floors to the street
he has landed on   face up
but only staring at the ceiling he gets up

to look down from the window
at crews   uncertain why they were called
staring back,   and as usual,
at a world uncertain why it itself is going on

She jumped from a luxury
apartment building he had always
wanted to afford to live in

was probably on his mind when he turned in
for the night. What stones
we pillow the drop of our head,

that egg, on
to sleep.
Thin, light as the shell is, the dream pushes hard
into flight, raw when it comes
down to landing.

All that could have happened
watches from the roadside what did
        happen by.

The dead stand at their wreck thankful to see that
in fact they can't   not yet   from here,   see it;
                    and rescue's there, but uncalled

for now.
The shadow on the shoulder—   the shift
the hitchhike transmigration one world back to its other

Night Writing

The word closest in pronunciation
To an ambulance's siren is "*wrong*."

Next to Nothing

Air seemed an unnaturally clear vacuum
as if last night's snow completely emptied
the space between its fall and the raw fissure
of fresh white sky freed in the ceiling,
light torn open even inside.
                              As if
what was left to breathe were not thin air
but finally nothing, everything escaped,
as the world would through a coffin's closing fall,
and this is that someone else's blank slate.

Someone who wakes switched to a different
unit, to a different ward, unsure
what has transferred over, of what is
following,   if what follows him is him.

And next breath is next to what   released
                    to go

Ghost Dance Song for the Bed Next to Mine

The whirlwind! The whirlwind!
The snowy earth comes gliding!
(Northern Paiute)

A white plate floated into notice
across the tray, a low slowly moving cloud;
where it set on the paper liner
must have drawn some kind of a horizon.
He couldn't tell the time of day except
by meal he was so out of it. The air hurt
                    beneath its fog.

The very air   is to say everything, say
so much it must have made a wall hurt
then; and air now, that everything, says nothing,
nothing hurts more than emptiness, alone, old,
cured long ago to die of something else.
A white plate floats in without notice.

A Sky of Ceiling, a Lone Cloud Its Fan

The way it grabs   to watch the eye
take up seeing, be at its beginning
of attention, to know that there are fresh
starts when you can see the blade a moment,

the ceiling fan's delay in that first glance
before it spins where it has been spinning
all along, it can be a start to watch
the slice of moment splice back into time.

I could only tell the hours by the meal
for weeks, feel them stall like appetite
or,   solid world not kept on my stomach,
come apart, throw part of me out with the pan,
make it hard to know where or what I am,
feel even once I'm fine I don't feel here.

Though no more confined to a sky of ceiling
and lone cloud its fan, I still am roomed
behind glass air that when same meets different
makes of them walled solarium worlds within
worlds, rooms, that seen through pass through the other,
turning blades blurred into a flat disk, the hemisphere.

Locus in Black Folktale

A white dog with no head, shining in the dark
like a bulb but not giving off any light to the tracks
met my father at a railroad he didn't know was there
when he got lost as a little boy coming home at night
he followed the dog and the tracks to where he knew
he was at
and never saw the dog or the railroad ever again
he thought he saw that white before when he was littler
on his mother's dress before she died and then they came north.
My dad liked ironed white shirts when he went out dressed
to gamble. He never lost anything we ever saw even in the dark
of his days.
I've never even seen a picture of that grandmother
What is there to see to take except where she took him

I Keep Arriving at a House That Isn't Mine

These drops, the cars' headlights along the wire
of the highway down off the hill aren't
the rain I hear beneath the wooded eaves
of the valley   These
pool into driveways beside a spout.

It mightn't even be the rain falling.
Water running down a utility wire beads
and rips loose into a driphead heard counterpoint
to rain
to the still note of the distant cars' image

to my own track of calm the rain is looped to play
as ambience through its phones   Instead:
the rain you can't hear to the edge of,
rain you listen for the splice horizon in
all the way through its soothe, and rain off

into something else   a gutter-
washer   a flash flood.   All of the above
forget their lives as each other's noise,
forget sound is one-directional   time, and repeat,
a fugue of echoes.

I keep arriving at a house that isn't mine.

I Didn't Mean

when it crossed my mind
So high, can't get over it
So low, can't get under
So wide, you can't get around
You must come in through . . .   **To**

Be   signifyin'. . .
I sat on the half of a seat left

beside her her bulk hadn't taken,
the late guest accepting what he gets.
Half of me in the aisle even sitting, not standing,
not an upper body just knees to step around.

I moved soon as another seat emptied
and she moved completely to the edge
and left the half seat a chock against the window
clearer

about size.   Always crowded,
always something in the way   to get around.

Gospel

A men's barbershop quartet
alto of a propeller plane
sound   over a bass nowhere
near that cheery   up
above my head   harmonizes

darkness on a set with
the light of day   a brush fire
of boater hats and stripes a kid
flying solo back to classes
plane runs out of gas over the lake   ice

a mayday five miles from the lights
of Chicago the lake 28
miles across   such
that anytime I hear a solitary
single engine through the last of dark
nearing the shore I can't help

feeling come on come on make it
though it's all gone down
already silent   I can feel it
still feel it in that sound lord
what shall I do

Seated Woman

Seated woman told the standing woman she could have her seat,
That she was getting off after the next two stops.
When the seated woman stood and tried to step aside so
The woman standing could maneuver round her to her seat,
A man on his phone moved to let her stand and took the seat.
The two women both now standing caught their balance
Falling against each other for a moment. The one about to
Get off said to the other, "I'm sorry." Her words
Became a public apology when an older three-eye woman
Said, "It's OK, baby. This is public transportation here,"
And put us all in this here place such   we all wanted off.
Obeah woman make us all sorry-
ass so
And so   *O Mayree dontchu weep* (Mahalia in our earphones)

The Good Woman Forgives God His Being

She wore a faint perfume of pain relievers
on her which she didn't seem old enough
to have earned   except somewhere in her eyes
the break there's no rub or plaster for
you can see shift the light.
She stares with the tightness of gritted teeth.
A glimpse gets through that says she'd never strike
again though   if ever she did.   she stays the right.

How could a god have so disappointed
one of its strong   what god-held weakness gave
way before her   for her to witness an act
of god as act rather than spirit?
You sense   the good woman she was before
something happened   that she still is   in her.
But that is hers   not anyone else's.   not god.
A cost for which she has paid in forgiving.

Drawing the Hand

(M. C. Escher)

    Of the mail,
the return portion's "Keep for . . ."
    left lying around—
readies for the poem (divergent response).

    The arriven envelope
opens space on its back
    for incoming,
anything at hand for anything
    to write on:
            problem
on or peep at
    a hand (never dealt done)
never starts out whole
    on one sheet of paper.

Always it's crap
    copied to the lined pad
that finger tap
    dances onto the big screen.

 Discovery's overnight
    star found at the drugstore
soda fountain myth
    is honest only

with its unexpected bit
    of torn off
slip the couch is   included.
    That the world is scribbled on

the cuff of the world,
    the poem is up its sleeve
with no idea it swears how
    it got there.

Was There

Not abandoned but been away from
a long time but then not really a place—

had dances for everything even before feet
has trees get up and strut the wind like it a street

make a stone talk—   the ground make sense
know when it start where lost or forgotten goes—

knows why I'm here—   and how this far is back
again   how worn away stripped clean complicates

as much as a callous   road-dirt scabs us up and that
there is a balm in Gilead on the times

square shuttle from a street musician's flute
can lift this all away to such silence

no one moves to get off the train

The words come up   between the blanks
But it's the silences   that string together
In something   like sentences
You have
              to   be not listening to hear

There's nothing   in the sentencing
That belongs   The words come up between

Something you have   and whatchamacallit
What you may call it   isn't a word

Between the blanks   that string together
Like sentences   be ye not listening to hear
In the sentencing   the words come up between

The words come up   but it's the silenced
In something you have   though nothing
Belongs   that belongs

The Edge

The toes of my hand step repeatedly
on the keyboard. I am going somewhere
with this. It's funny,
but I don't remember wearing
what formed these opposable bunions.
The clubs, hammers, and screwdrivers
must have fit around
what turned things out. Otherwise,
my thinking would be all air like a bird's,
all my brains, stripped back for the weight,
in the muscles, or it could be water
on my brain instead, anyway I'm here
pacing off ideas into objects,
but often also into thin air.

Spring as the Comics Section

Trimmed back to stick marks
of Xs on the ground,
they remind me where the color
will return in a couple months;

but then—that row of bloom—
how could I miss such ruckus,
just short of breaking a heart's bones,
had it any.
         Some say
it's been a rough year,
just short of putting –

as in cartoons—those Xs
in for eyes that flower here
—as if that's how
you pronounce dead

American Goldfinch

The bob of goldfinches   along
        the ripples of wind
    between the budding trees
             splashes of yellow

the way they fly
       as sudden a drop
   as bounce   back in the air
           the stone of their black

skipping
       the way they arrive
   each year   a rush
           that separates, fading

each into the leaves of its season
        'til migration.
   Birds and butterflies, souls,
             the souls of great warriors

in Mayan thought,
     but who
   would skip gold pieces
           across the water

against their flight?

The Following Moment (Spain)

Ahead of its corner, the visible
shadow of someone you can't see
on the other side of a sunlit wall
from this slant

shade   leans into view, a gnomon
announcing
the following moment

come,   called or not
No dog. But a tail

doggedly of
that end,   result

come of it   it's called.
Or not.

Dog without a head,
but such a glow of eyes

as to blind a head from sight.

One moment disappears into another:
to live is in the following.

A shish kebab of horizons
only showing,   where they were pierced,
the wavy extent of Salvador Dali's mirage: legs.
Elephants on dotted stilts

Follow the subtle distortions
left behind on the potential   between
those disappearances.

Transporte Mixto

Two extra seats welded to the frame
of the truck cab make this business
not tourism   though what we've seen
all morning   no screen but the world
itself could take on and even a peep
through don't-look-fingers would fill theaters

Every space to sit   on top of the load
is occupied by its farmers looking instead
to market not the mountains the one lane
thousand foot drop off over the pass way
you do business   even in the face
of another truck's sudden rounding the corner

You don't speak the language you do
speak with common eyes   that face we
let speak all at once as one   recognition
No one has to
repeat that silence's sound   The cost of business
is something more than the experience

than the view. More
like the women who appear with warm bread
out of nowhere when a landslide moments ahead
closes the road
or like the thought of having to eat
our words for fear to deal.

Untitled

Some movement, sail, propeller, oar, stops.
One road ends at another,   a harbor.
Water at land, land at the roadside-less distance
of crossing. Like puddles, the last footprints
of the sea's way in the dirt, of earth on the water, the harbor.

This is cargoes' water, not that longer blue, and the landscape
is for landing and unloading,
an end for disembarking to start   here new.
But the harbor started new its patience of rock
with shuttling wave and knows there is no stopping here,

only being turned around, turning back
to the beginning even at the start. As the waves wheel
round and turn   to sand the harbor
the harbor knows   to lose it all, it will receive it all   back,
the gold that even far beyond the journey has a trade longer than life.

This sheltering arc
is patient, it sends you away a spring to have you sent back Styx.
The sun grinding sparkles off the water burnishes black
the sea cherubs swimming out to bring in the arrivistes:
these tossed pennies. The continent still due the bones of its ship.

Shadows of shoals, of basalts, swimmers
stroking rhythmically as waves out to something
they think they see afloat.

Instrument

for Kristiana Rae Colón

In some of the recordings you can hear the walls' thing
with the bass how plastered
into structurally not moving they give back all the room

the robbed perspective drunks leaning into the wall lose,
transfer in a buttress of stone-face listening
room back into the sound of the room, into the song

so deep the sound feels come from underground,
up the cellar stairs. Bottle. Vibration at the root of the dead.
Who to cry for? The empty corner, furnished in dirt

is a hollow we pack in at the bottle of that
drum the walls seat in, the earth has jar. Tap it
tap out   it's living

Ed Roberson is the author of nine books of poetry, most recently *To See the Earth Before the End of the World* (2010), which was a finalist for the 2010 Los Angeles Times Book Prize and one of two runners-up for the 2011 Kingsley and Kate Tufts Poetry Award. His other honors include the 2008 Shelley Memorial Award from the Poetry Society of America and the 2011 Stephen Henderson Critics Award for Achievement in Literature. He is currently Distinguished Artist in Residence at Northwestern University, where he teaches in the Creative Writing Program.